BARRY WATTS

The Amazing Magic Book

ILLUSTRATIONS: MARK DAVID

Angus&Robertson
An imprint of HarperCollins*Publishers*

The Road to Magical Success

Becoming a good magician is very much like being the tortoise in the race against the hare — if you practice hard, eventually your progress will amaze everyone. But if you just want to have a bit of fun now and again, there are easy tricks that can be quickly mastered.

There are no short cuts to becoming a good magician, but there are a few simple rules which you should follow:

- Practice each trick until you know it thoroughly
  — then practice it again, and again.

- The "secret" of most tricks is amazingly simple
  — they are your secrets, not to be told to anyone.

- Keep your audience in front of you, not at the sides or behind
  — if your audience surrounds you, ask them to move (and do not begin until they do).

- Never perform a trick you are unsure of or feel uncomfortable with
  — if you feel unsure of a trick, you are more likely to make mistakes with it.

- Never tell your audience what you are going to do in advance
  — create an air of suspense and keep the surprise until the end.

- Learn your patter thoroughly and rehearse it well
  — know all the steps in sequence and the words that go with them.

- Never repeat any trick to the same audience
  — this only increases their chance to spot your secret.

- Use your face and gestures to dramatize the tricks
  - use frowns and stares to aid your concentration.
  - stand perfectly still and silent to gain attention.
  - use flourishes and sweeping movements with your wand to accentuate your magic powers.
  - use arm and hand movements to distract attention (see the section on Patter).

Use frowns and stares

Stand still

Use sweeping movements and flourishes with your wand

- Check all your equipment before you perform
  - make sure everything is ready to work and don't leave anything up to others to do for you.

- Add your own ideas to old tricks
  - if some methods seem awkward to you, adapt them to suit you better. Perhaps you can run

several of them together and create a totally new effect.

- Never perform with the light behind you; find a dark background
  - light can reveal secrets and distract attention.

Choose a dark background

wrong

Right

Cultivating Your Magic Powers

There are eight steps in learning to be a good magician:

1

Read this book through and choose a trick that seems easy to learn. Study the instructions and drawings carefully. Write down each step, one under the other, on a piece of paper. (This will help you remember it.) Do not try to learn all the tricks at once.

Write down each step

2

Slowly perform the whole trick, step by step, saying your patter over to yourself. If you make a mistake, just go back and start again until it comes right.

3

Avoid taking short cuts. Once you feel you've got all the steps right, repeat the trick right through several times — this will improve your confidence and help you to coordinate the words and actions.

4

Learn which movements you have to disguise (if any) and remember the places where you will have to "misdirect" your audience's attention. Once you feel comfortable with the new trick, stand in front of a full-length mirror and perform it to yourself. Watch closely and make sure all your movements are smooth and natural. Look for any weaknesses that your audience might see, and find a way to overcome these.

Practise in front of a mirror

5

Even when you've learnt the trick thoroughly and practiced it over and over (and even performed it to an audience), keep practicing it. The best magicians are those who practice their tricks even when they seem to be doing them perfectly.

6

Gradually build up your range of tricks. Mix up the type of tricks you perform so your audience has a variety of entertainment — for example, a card trick and some mental magic followed by a rope trick, a coin disappearance and, say, a trick with numbers.

7

Keep practicing.

8

Even when you can perform your routine perfectly (and you've learnt all the sequences, movements and patter by heart), practice some more!

Patter

Patter is the name given to the words spoken by a magician during a performance. Sometimes these are simple jokes or explanations; at other times it is the magic chant "Hocus pocus", which indicates the climax of a trick.

Patter is very important to a magician. It helps the performer stay in charge of the audience's attention.

DISTRACTING ATTENTION

"Bim Sala Bim!" shouts the magician, flinging his right hand high in the air.

Meanwhile, with his left hand, he is quietly removing something from his trouser pocket, unseen. The audience will concentrate on his raised right hand for two important reasons. Firstly, because the magician, too, is looking at his right hand and the audience usually looks where the performer looks. Secondly, raising the right hand in a

quick movement draws attention to it.

This simple example of patter, combined with body movement, shows how a magician directs his audience's attention away from actions that he does not want seen.

CONFUSING YOUR AUDIENCE

Patter is also used by the magician to remind the audience of what they have just witnessed, particularly when the magician is about to change things. "We've just seen the red ball under the middle cup," he might say, when that is the impression the magician wants his audience to have. He has, however, already moved the red ball elsewhere, unseen.

MISDIRECTING ATTENTION

The next use of patter is to guide the audience towards reaching the wrong conclusion, another

verbal skill practiced by magicians. For example, as the magician reaches towards a bottle of lemonade, he says, "And now we take this bottle you just saw me empty..."

This reinforces the idea that the audience did see the magician empty the bottle, and exaggerates the surprise when the magician pours even more lemonade from it!

Try to develop your own patter to suit the range of tricks you perform, and the speed with which you present them. This is far better than copying another magician's words.

TIMING

Timing is a very important part of patter, too, just as it is with the tricks themselves. When you are practicing your tricks, run through the words aloud, as well.

"Bim Sala Bim!"

This is the cry, the chant, the incantation that helps your magic work — or at least we pretend it does! You can invent your own group of nonsense words if you like. There is a magician who always says: "Hocus pocus, tin-canned onions!" and his tricks always work.

With the following card trick, however, it is necessary to chant "Bim Sala Bim", because it contains the right number of letters to make the trick work properly.

You will need:

- A pack of cards.

EFFECT:

1

Deal out three piles of seven cards, face down. Have a member of the audience select one pile, which you pick up and fan, so that the audience (and not you) sees the cards. The same person then chooses one card in the fan and points it out to the audience. They know it, but you don't.

2

Put all the cards into a pile (making twenty-one) and use them to make a further three piles of seven cards. This time, each pile is fanned to the audience, and they indicate the one with the previously selected card in it.

Yep! That one.

6

3

Repeat this procedure once more, then cast your spell, "Bim Sala Bim", over the twenty-one-card pile and, putting one card on the table for each letter called, spell out B-I-M S-A-L-A B-I-M.

As if by magic, the very next card (the eleventh) will be the one chosen by the spectator.

THE SECRET:

Follow this procedure and the trick will work by itself. Always deal the cards out one at a time from left to right to make three piles. The chosen pile (the one containing the selected card) is always put in the middle (between the two unchosen piles), before the recounting starts. Never shuffle the cards.

After the third time the pile has been nominated and is back between the others, just spell out "Bim Sala Bim" and turn over the next card.

1 Always deal the cards out from left to right.

1st pile (left)   2nd pile   3rd pile (right)

2

The chosen pile always goes in the middle (between the unchosen piles)

3 After the 3rd time the chosen card is always the 11th card!

Make Your Own Magic Wand

Every magician needs a magic wand to help him present his tricks to maximum effect. Here's how to make one — with some special built-in magic of its own!

You will need:

- A 35 cm (14 in.) length of curtain dowel made from plastic-coated tubing about 1.5 cm (½ in.) in diameter.
- About 60 cm (24 in.) of white hat elastic.
- Two beads, same color and slightly larger than the diameter of the curtain dowel (buttons may be used instead).

1

Check to make sure the ends of the curtain dowel are smooth. If they are sharp or jagged, file them down until they are smooth. Thread the first bead with the hat elastic and poke the end of the elastic through the tubing.

2

Thread the second bead onto the other end of the elastic. Stretch the elastic back through the tubing and knot the ends together.

By experimenting with the following trick, you can establish if the elastic is too loose or too tight. Adjust the length of the elastic so the trick works comfortably.

curtain dowel

2 beads or buttons.

← hat elastic

1

Poke the elastic through the tube

2

secure second button

3

8

The Master's Wand

EFFECT:

1

Hold your wand upright in your right hand, with the bottom of the wand level with your little finger.

2

Pushing down on the top of the wand with your left hand, force the wand through your closed fist until the top of the wand is level with the top of your fist.

Now, placing your left hand 15 cm (6 in.) below the bottom of the wand, the magician appears to exert an invisible force as the wand gently rises without being touched by your left hand.

THE SECRET:

Just as the left hand pushes the wand down through the closed right fist, the right little finger crooks around the bottom bead and holds firm, stretching the elastic as the wand is pushed down.

On command (when the grip is loosened in the right hand), the wand rises to the original position as if by magic. The left hand only appears to influence it!

wand rises to original position

little finger hooks around button

REMEMBER!

Make sure nobody hears the bead or button returning against the metal at the end of this trick.

Keep some extra hat elastic available for replacement, as the edge of the curtain dowel may cut the stretched elastic.

PATTER:

"Watch closely as I demonstrate the magical powers of this simple wand. We'll push it down through my clenched hand," (crook your little finger around the bottom bead as you do it) *"and hold it firmly."*

"Now, exercising my invisible magic powers, watch the wand respond to my left hand." (Gently release your right-hand grip and raise your left hand slowly under the end of the wand.) *"Hey presto, it's magic!"*

Arm Stretch

This is a simple and effective illusion which requires no advance preparation and just a little practice.

EFFECT:

1

Stand still with your left hand level with your waist. With the thumb and forefinger of your right hand, pinch the loose skin on the back of your left hand, near the knuckle of the middle finger.

2

After shaking the loose skin, the magician appears to stretch the length of the left arm by tugging it out of its sleeve for an extraordinary length.

THE SECRET:

This trick only works if you're wearing a loose coat or jacket (one without a snug-fitting wrist).

The secret is to make the coat sleeve stay still by pressing it against your body with your wrist as the right hand tugs the skin.

The elbow of the sleeve must remain in the same position, but your own elbow moves slowly through the lower sleeve to create the "stretched" effect.

To conclude the trick, clench the left fist and tap your left fingers with your right hand, as you gradually ease your left arm back into its normal position.

PATTER:

"I was taught this trick by a man from Longreach in outback Queensland . . . boy, did he have a long reach! Watch how he did it. He simply s-t-r-e-t-c-h-e-d his arms, like this," (only do the effect to one arm, though) "reached across the table for whatever he wanted, shrunk them back to normal like this," (tap fist and arm back into sleeve) "and got on with whatever he was doing. Some outback Queenslanders have terrible table manners!"

REMEMBER!

Remove all watches, bangles and bracelets from your left arm before beginning this trick.

Again, practice this by standing in front of a mirror and observing the effect

press the sleeve against you here

Dinky Dice

You will need:

- Three dice.
- A pen and notepaper.

EFFECT:

1

Introduce the three dice, and the pen and notepaper. Ask a volunteer from the audience to roll the three dice, while you stand at the back of the stage, facing away from the audience. Ask for the dice to be picked up in any order and stacked on top of each other.

2

Still with your back to the audience so you cannot see the action, instruct the volunteer to add up the numbers of the five hidden faces of the dice. Then ask the volunteer to write the number down and silently show it to the audience.

3

The paper with the answer on it is then torn up and the magician, turning to the audience for the first time, moves towards the front of the stage and, seemingly by mental telepathy, correctly announces the answer.

THE SECRET:

The opposite sides of a dice will always add up to seven. The opposite sides of three dice therefore add up to twenty-one.

When the magician turns and steps forward he simply glances at the number on the top of the top dice and subtracts it from twenty-one. Hey presto, he has the correct answer! For example, if he sees a four, he knows the five hidden faces add up to twenty-one less four — that is, seventeen.

The act of not facing the audience, of tearing up the written answer and of struggling for the mental answer is simply showmanship and has nothing to do with reaching the correct answer.

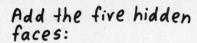

Add the five hidden faces:
1: Bottom of top dice
2: Top of middle dice
3: Bottom of middle dice
4: Top of bottom dice
5: Under bottom dice

Domino Prediction

Like many good tricks, this one is deceptively simple. To help its presentation, the magician should exaggerate the amount of concentration required to make it work — touching his forehead with eyes closed, for example.

You will need:

- A pen and notepaper.
- An envelope.
- A bag containing domino tiles.

EFFECT:

Write a prediction on a piece of notepaper, then seal it in an envelope and give to a member of the audience to hold. Introducing the bag full of dominoes, ask for a volunteer to set them out on the floor as if playing the game.

When the volunteer has finished, ask him to announce the numbers of the dominoes at each end of the line (for example, five and two).

The envelope containing the prediction is then opened by the spectator, who is asked to read aloud the contents. "I predict that the numbers at the ends of the row will be five and two," he will announce. Absolutely correct!

THE SECRET:

One domino is removed from the set before they are introduced. In this example, it was the five/two. Take any domino you like away, but never a double. Don't let anyone see you remove it, and do not allow others to count the number of dominoes used.

Remember the numbers on the missing domino, as you have to use them in your "prediction". It doesn't matter which one you take, it will always correspond with the end numbers, as long as you remember not to take a double away.

Magic Mail

You will need:

- A pen and notepad.
- An envelope.

EFFECT:

1

Introduce your props. Write a figure on the pad, tear off the page and seal it in the envelope. Then call on the audience to nominate any spectator among them to come forward to help with the next trick. When the volunteer steps forward, first give him the sealed envelope to put in his pocket for safekeeping.

2

The volunteer is then given the pen and pad and asked to add up four figures. They are:

- The year of his birth.
- The year he started school.
- His age at the end of this year.
- The number of years since he started school.

3

When he has finished the sum, ask him to open the envelope. He will find the magician has already written the same answer and sealed it in the envelope!

THE SECRET:

The answer will always be twice the current year. For example, if this trick was done by a ten-year-old in 1990, the sum would be:

- Year of birth 1980
- First went to school 1985
- Age 10
- Years since he first started school 5

Total   3,980

3,980 is exactly twice 1990! Try it yourself.

REMEMBER!

Never repeat this feat to the same audience. They will quickly realize you've given the identical answer.

For an adult volunteer, use "year he was married" instead of "year he started school", and "number of years since he married" for "years since he started school". The answer will remain the same.

They find the answer in the sealed envelope

1980+
1985
10
5

3,980

3,980

15

Thumbs Away!

If you can learn and practice this trick until you've mastered it, you'll have an impromptu illusion that will last you a lifetime and continue to amaze new audiences. Foreign children can be amused with it, even if they don't speak your language.

EFFECT:

The tip of your left thumb is magically removed from your hand.

THE SECRET:

By cleverly bending both your left and right thumbs at the knuckle and placing them together (the join covered with the right forefinger), the illusion is given of a complete finger — but a finger that can be broken in two.

METHOD:

1

Hold your left hand in front of you, just above waist height. Have your palm towards your body, your fingers flat and pointing to the right. Bring your thumb into line with your forefinger.

2

Grab your left thumb with your right thumb and forefinger (finger towards your audience) from above. Pretend to be trying to pull the top off your left thumb.

1 As seen by the performer:

Bring left thumb in line with forefinger

magician's left hand

2

pretending to pull off the left thumb (as seen by the performer)

Aaagh!

3

Start again. This time, as you place your right forefinger over the left thumb knuckle, bend the top of your left thumb in and place your right thumb so it appears to replace it.

4

The next part is even harder for beginners. Tuck the last fingers of the right hand away, so your audience can clearly see your right thumb tip (which looks like it's your left thumb tip).

5

Now, to complete the illusion, hold your left hand still and slowly slide the right thumb along the top of your left forefinger. Then slowly slide it back to the original spot.

   As you perform these slides, move your elbow out from your body — this will stop people seeing parts of your thumbs which would reveal the secret.

6

As the thumbs touch, allow the tucked-up fingers to come forward as a screen, and separate your hands.

REMEMBER!

Practice this trick every day in front of a mirror for a whole month before demonstrating it to anyone.

3 Move right forefinger over right thumb knuckle

palm of left hand

Back of right wrist

4 As the audience sees it:

left hand

right hand

5

6 these fingers act as a screen

Acrobatic Money

You will need:

- A banknote, of any value.

EFFECT:

Invite the audience to watch closely as you fold the banknote.

Fold it three times and then unfold it, drawing attention to it having remained the right way up. The money is then re-folded in the same way, only to reveal, when it is unfolded, that is has turned upside down.

METHOD:

Start by holding the left and right edges of the note in an upright position, between your thumbs and forefingers of both hands. Face the audience.

1

Fold the top edge down towards you and crease the note in half lengthways.

2

Move the right edge frontward to the left edge, and crease the note again.

3

Fold the right half frontward again to the left, and crease it.

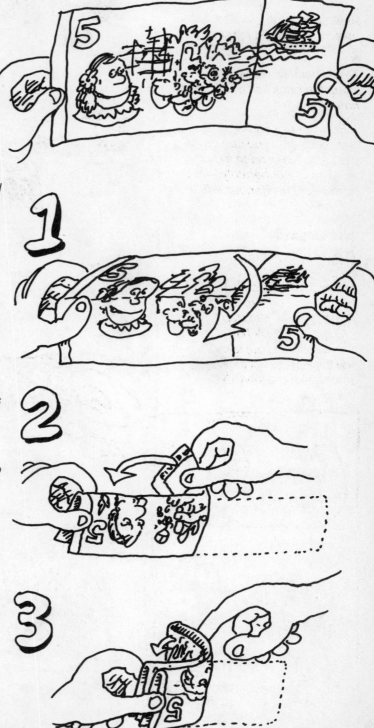

4

Now, unfold the back half of the note (the two doubled corners) by swinging them to the right.

5

Next, swing the front half of the note from the right to the left.

6

To get back where you started, lift up the back half of the folded note.

Practice this folding sequence until you can do it naturally. Make each move slowly and deliberately — this adds to the mysterious effect.

THE SECRET:

In the second sequence of unfolding the note (when you're making the note stand on its head), proceed through steps 1 to 4, then slightly alter step 5 by swinging the back half of the note (the half facing you) to the left. Lift the back portion of the note to reveal the topsy-turvy design.

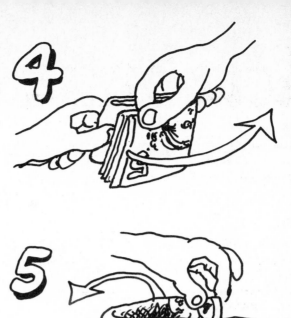

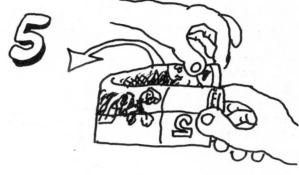

Now try to do it with this coin.

The Art of Concentration

This is a wonderful trick, but as you'll see, it must never be repeated to the same audience.

You will need:

- A local telephone book.
- A pen and notepad.

EFFECT:

Produce your props, then ask for a volunteer from the audience.

Announce that you will quickly memorize all the information in the telephone directory, and quickly scan through it, skipping some pages in haste. Then announce: "Right, I know every line now!"

Ask the volunteer to do some calculations and to announce the answer. Using figures from the answer, *you say, "Turn to page X of the phone book, look at the Nth name in the right column, but don't read it aloud."*

The magician puts his hand on his forehead, closes his eyes, and appears to concentrate his mental powers. He then announces the correct name and address from the telephone book entry — the volunteer confirms it is right.

METHOD:

1

First, get your local telephone book and turn to page eighty-nine. Checking the far right column only, run down to the tenth entry from the top and memorize the name and address (and the number, if you wish). Make sure you learn it perfectly.

Give the volunteer the notepad and ask him to write down any three different figures under ten. Ask him to reverse them and subtract the smaller one from the larger one. If his answer is less than a hundred, tell him to add a zero at the front.

Tell him to reverse the new answer and add the original number and the new number together. The answer will be 1089, but don't announce that.

2

Ask the volunteer to turn to the telephone directory page nominated by the last two figures (page eighty-nine) and to count down the right-hand column the number of entries indicated by the first two figures (ten).

Then, after you have shammed "concentration", announce the name and address and have it confirmed as correct.

first two figures

last two figures

THE SECRET:

If you write down three different numbers under ten, reverse them and take the smaller from the larger one, and then reverse that answer and add them together (follow the example shown so you understand it clearly), the answer will always be 1089.

That's why you memorized the tenth name in the right column of page eighty-nine — got it, 1089?

The Magic Ribbon

Even the smartest members of your audience will scratch their heads and wonder how you do this one.

You will need:

- An envelope.
- A pair of scissors.
- A length of ribbon.

EFFECT:

1
Hold up your props to the audience.

2
Seal the envelope and cut its ends off. Place the ribbon through the envelope so that the ends of the ribbon hang from both sides of the envelope.

cutting the ends off the envelope

1

Place the coin in the middle of the square of paper and bring the bottom edge up to within 3 cm (1 in.) of the top. Crease the fold into position.

2

Fold about 5 cm (2 in.) of both sides back away from you, and crease the edges.

3

Fold the top 3 cm (1 in.) back away from you — the coin appears to be contained within the package, but the top edge facing you is open.

4

Hold the packet aloft in your left hand and point to it with your right, saying: "All safely locked away now."

5

Tap the package on the table so that the coin can be heard inside.

6

Transfer the package to your other hand, picking it up at the top between right thumb and forefinger and swinging it upside down. Keep the back of your hand to the audience and allow the coin to slide into your right palm. Don't drop it!

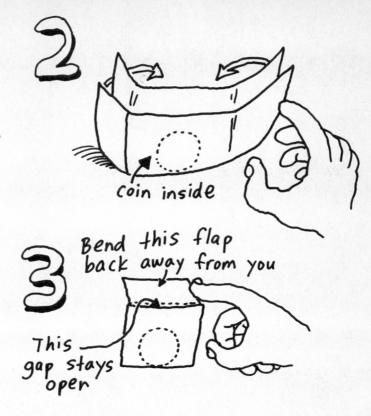

coin inside

Bend this flap back away from you

This gap stays open

All safely locked away now.

tap tap

coin slips into palm of right hand

7

Put the folded package back in your left hand and place it on the table. With your right hand, take your wand from your inside pocket, dropping the coin safely in your pocket.

8

Use the wand to cast a "disappearing spell" on the coin. Put the wand down, hold the package up and undo it, showing it to be empty. Tear the paper up so that no-one can follow your folding sequence.

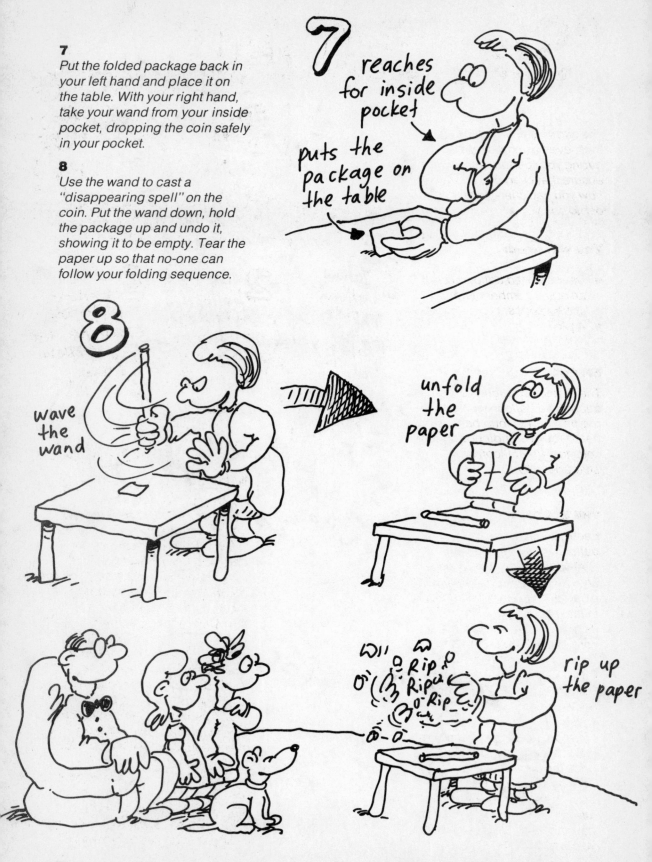

7 reaches for inside pocket

puts the package on the table

8

wave the wand

unfold the paper

rip up the paper

"Stay Awake!"

The surprise element of this trick, even when it's repeated during your performance, will ensure that everybody notices how you can change the color of balloons!

You will need:

- Dark-colored balloons and an equal number of light-colored ones.
- A pin.

EFFECT:

The magician touches a decorative balloon with his magic wand. A loud bang is heard, but the audience simply sees that the balloon has changed colors.

THE SECRET:

Each balloon has a second balloon inflated inside it.

Always fit a light-colored one (for example, yellow) inside a darker one (such as blue) and inflate the inner one first, tying its neck and securing it to the cord of the outer one with cotton.

Next, inflate the outer, darker balloon to create an air space between each balloon and tie its neck.

Tape a pin to one end of your magic wand. Use this end to prick the outer balloon.

If you should accidentally burst both balloons together, just say: "That should make you pay attention!" and go on with your act.

1 Yellow balloon inside the blue

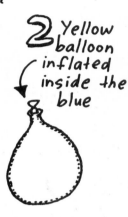

2 Yellow balloon inflated inside the blue

3 Blue balloon inflated around the yellow

METHOD:

Have, say, four dark blue balloons as decorations around the stage or room.

During the early part of your performance of other magic tricks, make some casual references about the balloons, just to make certain your audience is aware of their color, for example: "I'm pleased to have blue balloons, but I prefer yellow ones."

If the audience response to one of your tricks is not enthusiastic enough, just touch one of the balloons with your wand and, bang! — its color is changed from blue to yellow.

From time to time during your act, burst all the balloons in the same way and use comments like: "Wake up! Nobody goes to sleep during my performance!"

The Invisible Tear

You will need:

- A handkerchief.
- A large safety pin.

EFFECT:

Pierce a folded handkerchief with a large safety pin and move it along the fold without tearing the handkerchief.

THE SECRET:

Knowing how to insert and hold the large safety pin is the key to performing this correctly.

Practice on a piece of old cloth until you thoroughly understand the technique, otherwise you will tear borrowed hankies and make yourself very unpopular.

helper

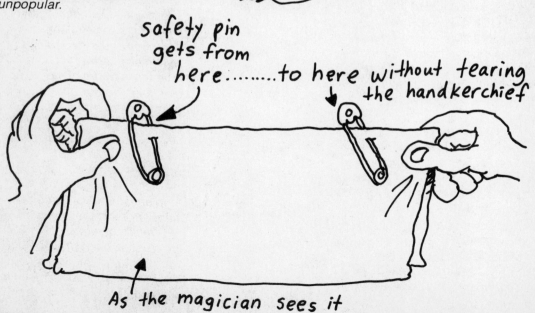

safety pin gets from here.........to here without tearing the handkerchief

As the magician sees it

METHOD:

Ask a spectator with a handkerchief to volunteer to help you. Have the helper stand facing you. Fold the handkerchief in half lengthways, and each hold an end near the fold. It is very important to keep the fold stretched tight.

1

Pierce both layers of the handkerchief with the pin near the fold at your end.

2

Clasp the loop of the pin firmly between your right thumb and forefinger, making absolutely sure that the cap end of the pin is on the left, so the pointed bar is on the right inside the cap.

3

In a sudden movement, pull down and along with your right hand, forcing the cloth around the point of the pin, inside the cap.

4

After you've moved the pin about 25 cm (10 in.), stop. With a quick upward movement, make the pin pierce the cloth again, and let go.

   Hey presto! You've magically moved the pin along the fold without causing a tear and with the pin apparently still closed!

1

2 (As the magician sees it)
← pointed bar

cap

cap end of the pin

hold the loop firmly

3

magician's left hand

4 magician's left hand

slide along . . . . .
and then stop
and jab up.

helper's hand

29

"Now You See It, Now You Don't"

This is a really effective trick which will surprise your friends. It calls for nimble fingers, body movement, some distracting patter and lots of practice. Professional magicians call it the "French drop".

EFFECT:

Hold any small object, such as a coin or key, in your left hand, and sprinkle it with magic "woofle dust".

Transfer it into the right hand and, hey presto, it disappears into thin air, only to be found again behind the performer's knee, or sometimes behind a spectator's ear.

THE SECRET:

As the object which disappears never leaves the performer's left hand, it is important that the magician creates the impression that he has transferred it to his right hand. If you follow these instructions carefully, you'll learn how to create that impression.

METHOD:

1

Hold the coin between the thumb and middle finger of your left hand, palm upwards and at waist height.

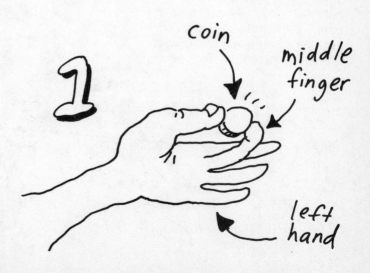

2

Tell your audience to watch the coin carefully: "I am going to sprinkle it with 'woofle dust' and give it magic powers."

3

Grab a handful of invisible "woofle dust" in your right hand and pretend to sprinkle it over the coin. ("Woofle dust" is always available to magicians, and is invisible. I've found that there's usually some about an arm's length in front of my right shoulder — you'll probably find some in front of yours, too.)

4

Hold your left hand steady and bring your right hand down. Make sure your thumb goes under the coin from behind and your right fingers obscure the coin from your audience.

5

Under cover of your right fingers, the coin falls into the palm of your left hand. (Do not wear a ring on any of your left fingers or the coin may make a noise and give you away!)

6

Continue the movement by closing your right hand as if it held the coin. At the same time, gently close your left fingers over the hidden coin.

2 I am going to sprinkle it with woofle dust.

3

4 left hand in same position as step 1.

right hand

right hand closed

6 coin inside fingers of left hand

5 coin in palm of left hand

7

All the movement should now be with your right hand. Look at your right hand as you move it, keeping the back of your hand facing the audience, to shoulder height. Move your right fingers as if squeezing the coin (which isn't there). Point towards the squeezing right fingers with the forefinger of your left hand.

8

Move your weight onto your left foot and, at the same time, slowly turn your body slightly to the right, watching your raised right hand all the time, still pointing towards it with your left forefinger.

9

Then, suddenly, stop the squeezing motion in your right hand. Swivelling your wrist so your palm faces your audience, fling your hand wide open, fingers apart. Tell your audience: "It's disappeared."

10

Ask them: "Where can it be?", while feeling around with your right hand behind a spectator's ear, as if trying to find the coin. Next, pretend to look for the missing coin, again with your right hand, behind your own right knee, by bending slightly. "Not there!", tell your audience, showing an empty right hand.

11

"Here it is!", you announce, as you reach with your left hand behind the ear of another spectator, pretending to remove it, although you and I know the coin was in your left hand all the time.

REMEMBER!

With this trick in particular, practice in front of a mirror is essential. Do not perform it until you are perfect in both word and action. Once you can do it properly, it will stay with you for the rest of your life, enabling you to amaze and amuse people anywhere. Do not repeat the trick to the same audience.

The Color-changing Pencil

Pencils and a handkerchief are used in this example, but as this trick is performed sitting down, you may use spoons and forks and a table napkin if you're doing it at the dinner table.

You will need:

- Two pencils, of different colors, or a fork and a spoon.
- A handkerchief or a square table napkin.

EFFECT:

Spread a handkerchief in a diamond shape in front of you, place a yellow pencil in the middle and fold the bottom corner to the top.

Roll the handkerchief towards you and ask a spectator to hold one corner pressed to the table.

The magician pulls the other corner, and reveals that the yellow pencil has turned blue!

THE SECRET:

Two pencils are used, one yellow and the other blue. The blue one is placed under the handkerchief, running from left to right, before the performer draws attention to the trick.

The pencil has changed colour.

handkerchief

blue pencil underneath

yellow pencil

METHOD:

1

Place the yellow pencil almost on top of the hidden one, and place the corner nearest you about 2 cm (¾ in.) short of the furthest corner, without drawing attention to it.

2

Place your palms over the covered yellow pencil and roll the handkerchief (including both pencils) under and towards yourself.

3

Allow corner B to rotate around the roll once. This is important if the trick is to work successfully.

4

Have a volunteer press a finger firmly on the corner B, while you take corner A and pull it swiftly towards yourself.

The hidden blue pencil will appear on top of the handkerchief, and the yellow one will roll onto your lap, out of sight.

REMEMBER!

The trick will be easier if there is a tablecloth on the table, so that the pencil underneath the handkerchief is less likely to make any noise.

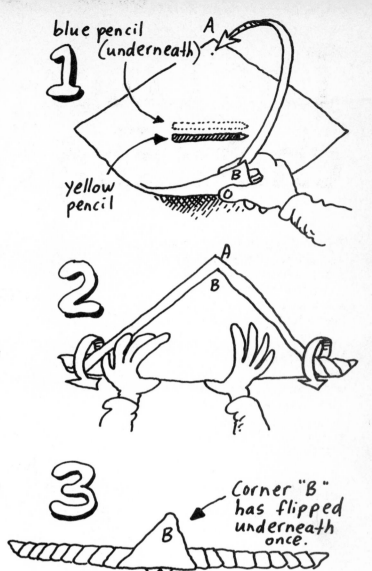

Jumping, Joining Paperclips

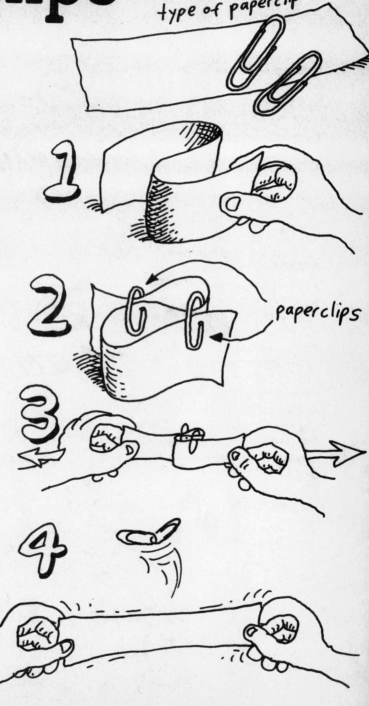

You will need this type of paperclip

You will need:

- A piece of colored paper measuring about 15 cm (6 in.) by 10 cm (4 in.).
- Two wire paperclips.

METHOD:

1
Bend the paper into an S shape.

2
Now add two paperclips in the positions shown. Add a sprinkling of invisible "woofle dust" and hold an end of the paper in each hand.

3
Say the magic words: "Bim Sala Bim," as, in one swift movement, you move your hands apart to straighten out the paper.

4
Presto! The paperclips will fly into the air, mysteriously joined together.

REMEMBER!

This trick will work without any preparation on your part — just follow the instructions and illustrations. (Plastic paperclips will not work.)

paperclips

"I Know Your Secrets!"

This is a clever and simple way to obtain someone's age and telephone number without them telling you.

You will need:

- Two pieces of notepaper and a pen.
- A calculator. (For 7-digit phone numbers you'll need a calculator with at least 9 digits.)

EFFECT:

Ask for a volunteer from the audience to help perform the next trick. Give that person two pieces of notepaper, a pen and a calculator, tell them to write down some information and then to do some silent calculations.

The final answer is written on a piece of paper and handed to the magician, who then announces the volunteer's age and telephone number.

THE SECRET:

The last two figures in the answer will be the age of the volunteer, and the first series of figures will be the telephone number.

If the second last figure is a zero, it means the volunteer is under ten years old and the last number is his age.

Tell the age first (the last two numbers) and then the phone number.

phone no.

×2

+5

×50

+age

+365

−615

METHOD:

Ask your volunteer to multiply his phone number by two, add five, multiply by fifty, add his own age, add 365, take away 615 — and there's the answer.

REMEMBER!

This trick is much more effective if you learn the sequence of instructions by heart.

Don't be tempted to repeat this trick again to the same audience. Once is enough to keep them guessing.

Magic Ping-pong Ball

"When Isaac Newton told the world about his law of gravity, he obviously didn't know about my magic ping-pong ball," the magician announces. "Now, watch closely."

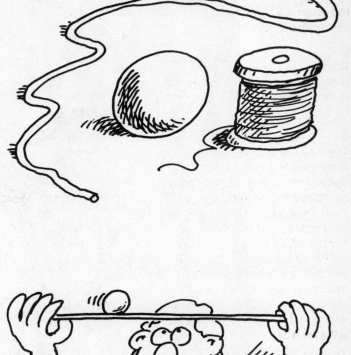

You will need:

- A piece of "sash cord" about 56 cm (22 in.) long, available from hardware shops.
- A table tennis ball.
- A length of white cotton, 60 cm (24 in.) long.

EFFECT:

Hold up a short length of rope horizontally and place a lightweight table tennis ball on it. As you tilt the rope from side to side, the ball gently rolls along the edge of the rope without falling off.

THE SECRET:

White cotton attached at each end of the sash cord and running along its length keeps the ball balanced.

METHOD:

1

Tie the cotton securely around the cord about 5 cm (2 in.) from one end. Allowing room to place your two thumbs between the cord and the cotton, run the cotton to within 5 cm (2 in.) of the other end of the cord, and tie as firmly as before.

2

When you pick up the rope, place your thumbs between the rope and the cotton, and keep both rope and cotton tight.

3

The ball is actually balanced between the rope and the cotton, which is hidden from the audience by the thickness of the rope. (Keep the cotton on your side of the rope.) By tilting your hands, while still keeping the rope and cotton tight, the ball will gently roll from one side to the other.

REMEMBER!

This is a wonderful trick, but it needs lots and lots of practice — particularly in picking up the ball between the thumb and finger at the start. (One magician I know puts the ball on the cord with his mouth. He says it's easy that way.)

This is a difficult trick to perform — tell your audience that, if you choose. Only run the ball up and back once, and then halfway again — don't attempt more than that.

Never do this trick if you are not at least 3 m (10 ft) away from your audience.

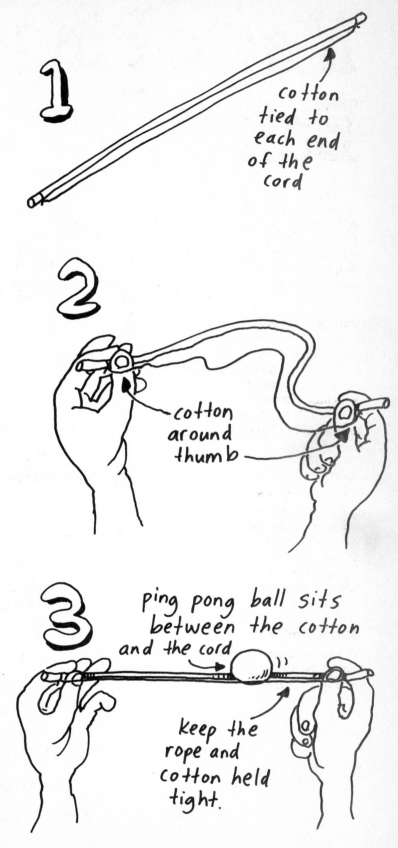

1

cotton tied to each end of the cord

2

cotton around thumb

3

ping pong ball sits between the cotton and the cord

keep the rope and cotton held tight.

The Disappearing Knot

You will need:

- A piece of thick string or thin cord about 30 cm (12 in.) long.
- A matchbox.

EFFECT:

Tie a simple knot around a matchbox cover, and pass one end of the string through the centre of the box.

Turning the box upright, push the knot along the cord — the knot will completely vanish!

THE SECRET:

The knot simply undoes itself when one end of the cord is passed back through the box and pulled.

METHOD:

1

Take the string or cord and tie a simple, single knot around the cover of the matchbox, so that one end leads off to the right.

The knot vanishes inside the matchbox cover

2

Now hold the matchbox cover upright and poke one loose end of the cord down through the center of the box. Have a volunteer from the audience hold the end that fell through the box.

3

Now gently slide the whole knot off the cover and push the knot into the box as well, letting the helper hold the other end in his free hand. Grasp the matchbox cover in your left hand, sprinkle it with invisible "woofle dust" and say the magic words: "Bim Sala Bim."

4

Ask the volunteer to gently pull the ends apart (which undoes the knot), and move the matchbox cover backwards and forwards to demonstrate that the knot has disappeared.

Hand the cord and matchbox cover out for inspection by the audience.

member of the audience holds this end

Tucking the knot into the box

volunteer holds both ends

slide the box along the cord

Rapid Card Telepathy

You will need:

- *A pack of cards.*

EFFECT:

Ask a spectator to shuffle the cards, and ask for complete cooperation from the audience so you can perform an amazing act of telepathy.

Holding the cards at arm's length, facing towards the audience, ask everyone to concentrate on the card at the front of the pack.

You then announce the correct card without seeing it.

After putting the pack behind your back ("So I can't see the next card," you say), bring another card to the front of the pack and hold it toward the audience. You correctly divine the next six cards in turn.

THE SECRET:

After the pack has been shuffled, put the pack behind your back and (unseen by the audience), take the top card, turn it over and move it to the back of the pack. Before beginning, announce something like: "This is what we're going to do . . . " and have a dummy run, without guessing the card this time, but memorising the card facing you

> It's a red card... mmm ... I think it's the ace of hearts ...

— it will be the card you "guess" first.

After you correctly name each card facing the audience, put the pack behind your back and move a new card to the front of the pack for your audience to concentrate on.

Each time you hold the pack up to the audience, you see, facing you, the card that is next to be shown to them. The audience assumes all the cards are facing towards them, but only the one facing them is.

magician's left hand

magician sees this card

audience sees the card facing them

METHOD:

Play the audience along — don't foretell the card immediately. Pretend to read their minds. Tell them it's a red card. A heart... a low-numbered heart. Stall a little, as if the picture you're getting is not clear. "It's not a two or a three... it's a four of hearts!" While you are doing this, look at the next card at the back of the pack, and remember it.

Don't run this trick for longer than six cards — that's enough to mystify the audience. Always tell them before the sixth card: "This is giving me a headache, we'll make this the last one."

... put the pack behind my back so I can't see the next card...

Mmm ... It's a black card ... spades ... yes ... it's the eight of spades.

The "Q" Card

You will need:

- A pack of cards.
- A pen and paper.

EFFECT:

Hand a pack of cards to a member of the audience, and ask for them to be shuffled. Ask for the pack to be cut in halves, and one half given back to you.

These cards are laid out on the table, face up, in the shape of the capital letter "Q".

You then produce a piece of paper and write something on it. Fold the paper over (so the message cannot be seen) and place it in the middle of the "Q".

Ask a member of the audience to count the number of cards in the "Q" by starting at the bottom of the tail and moving clockwise up the left side of the letter, touching each card and counting aloud, stopping whenever he likes.

Then, starting from the last counted card, ask him to count back around the "Q" to the same number, avoiding the cards in the tail, and going up the right side of the "Q", touching each card he counts.

All the cards, except the one at the end of this count, are removed from the table. When the volunteer is invited to read the message on the folded paper, he finds that although it was written before he started counting, it discloses the number and suit of the final card.

Have a member of the audience shuffle the cards

THE SECRET:

The counting will always finish as far up the right side as there are cards in the tail. For example, if there are six cards in the tail, the second count will end with the sixth card up on the right side from the tail. The name of that card is the one the magician writes down on the piece of folded paper at the beginning of the trick.

If you repeat this trick to the same audience (which is not recommended), make certain that you alter the number of cards in the tail to confuse your audience further.

You can use a big "Q" or a little "q". The trick will still work like magic. The number of cards in the tail doesn't matter, either. While you are learning to do it, though, I suggest you keep the number of cards down to half a pack.

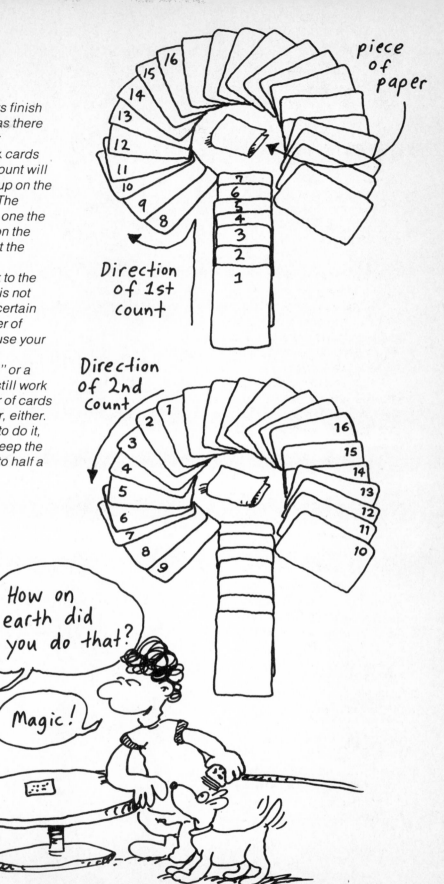

Counting
to Ten

This is a tricky little numbers trick. Like many tricks, once you know how to do it, everything is remarkably easy — but it is still very confusing for those who try to copy you.

You will need:

- *Three sugar cubes.*

EFFECT:

Start with three sugar cubes on a table, and count them aloud as you move them onto the palm of your left hand.

Then move them back onto the table while continuing to count up to six. Keep counting and put them back onto your palm, and then back onto the table while still counting.

You move the three cubes four times, but only count up to ten. When you ask members of the audience to count the sugar cubes as you did, they all fail.

METHOD:

Start with three cubes on the table. Pick up one lump and put it in your other hand and count "one". Put the next lump with the first and count "two". Next, the third lump joins the others with "three".

Now, one at a time, place them back on the table with "four", "five" and "six". Again,

... nine, ten.

Okay, see if you can count them as I did.

point to the table with your left hand

pick them up one at a time and count only as far as "seven" and "eight", then pause.

Just touch the cube that would have become "nine", but don't pick it up or say anything.

Take the two from the palm of your hand, one at a time, put them beside the one on the table and count "nine" and "ten". Everyone will know, or eventually work out, that you fudged the "nine" count.

So, just pick up the three sugar cubes and put them in a spectator's hand, point towards the table, and invite the spectator to count the cubes as you did.

He will fail, and so will everybody else you give the cubes to.

THE SECRET:

As you do the trick, you count as you pick up the sugar cubes. Because you hand them to the spectator to count, they will count the lumps as they are put down and be unable to fudge the "nine" count as you did.

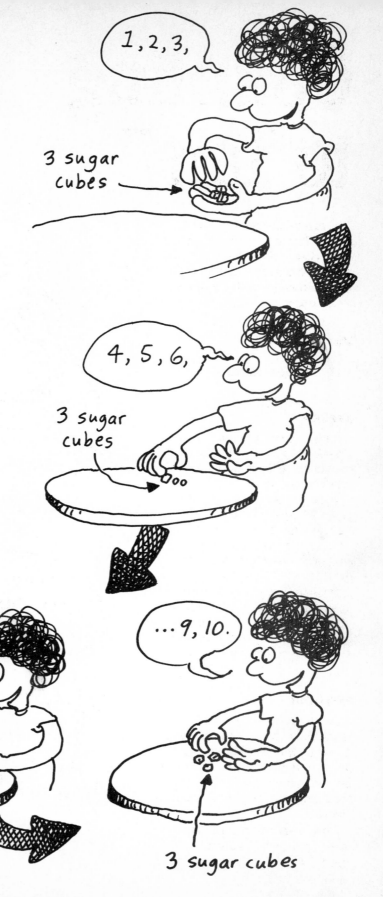

47